First published in the UK by Shanway Press
Copyright © 2016 by Daniel Mulholland
The Author asserts the moral right to be identified as the author of this work.
ISBN: 978-1-910044-10-0
Printed and bound in Great Britain by Shanway Press.

All rights reserved no part of this publication may be reproduced in a retrieval system, or transmitted in any form by any means, electronically, mechanical, photocopying or otherwise, without the prior permission of the publishers.

This book is sold subject to the conditions that it will not, by way of trade or otherwise, be lent, re-sold or otherwise without the publishers prior consent in any form of binding or cover other than that which it is published and without a similar condition including this condition being imposed on the subsequent publisher.

*I wish to thank Brian Lennon SJ
and Maria Mulholland BL
for their invaluable help.*

CONTENTS

Prologue 5

PART ONE
Chapter One: Taking stock 7
Chapter Two: Making sense of our thinking 9
Chapter Three: A model of thought 12
Chapter Four: Five steps 13
Chapter Five: Barriers to thinking 20
Chapter Six: Past experiences and knowledge 22
Chapter Seven: The role of the ego 24
Chapter Eight: Recognising the need to change 26
Chapter Nine: Thinking design faults 28
Chapter Ten: Thinking in story mode 30
Chapter Eleven: Surprising thoughts 33
Chapter Twelve: Thinking about me 36
Chapter Thirteen: Thinking about work 39
Chapter Fourteen: Thinking about possessions 41
Chapter Fifteen: Thinking about friendship 43
Chapter Sixteen: What thinking frames your life 45
Chapter Seventeen: Thinking about what you want 48

PART TWO
Chapter Eighteen: Thinking about the past 51
Chapter Nineteen: Thinking about the present 53
Chapter Twenty: Thinking about the future 55
Chapter Twenty-one: Six-day programme of discovery 57
Chapter Twenty-two: A new beginning 66

Epilogue 68

PROLOGUE

"There are three classes of people: those who see. Those who see when they are shown. Those who do not see."

– *Leonardo Da Vinci*

The ability to think is one of our greatest gifts. It may also be the gift we are least aware of. Thinking just seems to happen. Often our thinking – the programming, the belief systems, the finely tuned ego that helps shape our lives, appears to run on auto-pilot.

The thoughts we have are personal to us. Thinking is what makes me, me, and you, you. It not only determines who we are and what we do, it also determines who we become. Our thoughts are the compass that guides our lives. Independent thought gives us great freedom. Closed thinking can make us a prisoner of our own mind.

This book sets out to reflect on what we are doing when we are thinking. Using a simple model it will help you realise what is happening just outside of your awareness, begin to understand why you have the thoughts you do and how your life experience and actions are the result of the quality of your thinking.

Brian Keenan, a hostage in Beirut for five years, on his release from captivity said, "I was always a free man." For him his guards were the ones in prison. Their thinking made them prisoners of their ideology. They were incapable of escaping how they saw the world.

We all can end up in these thinking prisons with invisible bars. The challenge is to recognise our thinking patterns and break free. I hope to help you realise that most of what you hold to be true may in fact be an illusion. Recognising that will allow you to set yourself free and begin living the life you will love.

Chapter One
TAKING STOCK

"Faced with the choice between changing one's mind and proving that there is no need to do so, almost everyone gets busy on the proof."

– John Kenneth Galbraith

There is a story about the navy who lost a submarine. When a reporter asked their spokesperson if the submarine was lost, he responded by saying they could not say if it was lost or not. He went onto say that it was only when they found it would they be able to say whether it was lost or not. He went on to explain that although they had lost contact with the submarine and did not know where it was, if they found it where it was meant to be then the submarine would not be lost. If they found it somewhere it wasn't meant to be then they would consider it lost.

Our experience of life can be similar. We feel safe and content in what we are doing. Life appears good. We are relatively content with our lot. There is nothing in our awareness to indicate anything different.

Sometimes a single event can change all that. These unsettling events often happen when we least expect them. We do not see them coming. This can be in the form of an illness, redundancy, an accident or the sudden death of a loved one.

Nassim Nicholas Taleb, the writer, has described these events as 'black swans'. He uses the example of the turkey that is fed and looked after every day by the farmer. There is nothing in the turkey's everyday experience to suggest that the farmer, who has cared for and protected it, will one day soon chop off its head and eat it.

Habit is what can fool us. What we do on a regular basis becomes normal behaviour. When we have a particular recurring thought or repeat a particular action we are creating and establishing connections in our brain. These connections can be very useful as they form the programming for our everyday actions. Every time you get in the car you do not have to figure out how to drive it. You have repeated the experience often enough to lay down the mental pattern that allows you to drive without much thought. However thinking patterns whilst they are often very useful can sometimes be unhelpful and difficult to change.

We often tend to miss the thinking and live on auto-pilot. A simple question would be to ask when the last time we heard our footsteps. The answer may give us an indication of just how much we all operate on auto-pilot.

Ask any smoker is it easy to quit cigarettes? Any ingrained mental pattern takes a monumental effort to change. It is not only the addiction to nicotine that a smoker has to break. They also have to break the smokers' thinking pattern. Martin Laird, in his book 'Into the Silent Land' suggests that all activity in life including drug addiction, alcoholism, retail therapy, ambition, hobbies etc. are just an attempt to quiet the questioning mind; that part of us that knows we are capable of more. But where do these thinking patterns emerge from?

Our thinking began in infancy when we didn't fully realise what was happening. The ability to think came to us over a long period of time. As a result it now appears automatic. Something we do not give much attention to. Now lets take a closer look at this thing we call thinking.

Chapter Two
MAKING SENSE OF OUR THINKING

An old man was walking between two towns when he met a young man walking towards him. As they were passing the young man asked: "What is the town like I am walking towards?" the old man replied, "What is the town like you just left?"

Scientific understanding of thinking suggests that as little as 10% of what we see when we look out at the world is visual information. Our picture of the world is a construct of our brain's processing not a true account of what is actually there. Our brain collates the information from our senses, our expectations, our belief systems, past experiences and constructs an image of the world based on all of these.

This flow of thought never stops. We are continually bombarded with stimuli and are always busy trying to make sense of it all. Anyone who has tried to meditate will be aware of how busy the mind can be. Awake or asleep, like a river, our mind is in constant flow.

Just as our heart beating keeps us alive our thinking helps us navigate and make sense of this experience we call life.

Our mind creates our reality. That 'reality' is ours alone. It belongs to no-one else. It can be a startling realisation when you recognise that the world you live in is unique to you. It is wholly, completely and utterly yours.

Whilst our life is populated by many people, only one inhabits our mind, us. No one else will ever have the thoughts we have, feel the feelings we do or perceive the world like us. Just as our individual DNA is unique, our thoughts are also.

To use the computer analogy, we all have similar hardware – a brain, but the software running in there is different. We may have had a similar education, cultural and social conditioning but essentially we all run different software programs that influence how we perceive and experience life.

Our brains are extremely effective at interpreting the world. Steven Pinker in 'How the Mind Works' claims "The engineering problems that we solve as we see, walk, plan and make it through the day are more complex than landing on the moon or sequencing the human genome."

Because we get so much information from our senses one of the key functions of the brain is to filter. We can only hold one thought at a time. If we did not filter information effectively we would have great difficulty in living our lives. It would be impossible to exist in cities if we could not filter out most of the information. Take for example someone who lives close to a busy road. In time they will no longer 'hear' the traffic. Their brain has chosen to filter out the traffic noise.

So thinking has many practical applications and having the ability to process and manage the complex world we inhabit is an amazing skill. But have you ever asked yourself why you have the thoughts you do? Why this mind of yours does what it does?

Now a simple thought experiment. Suppose you and your best friend have just been arrested and are being questioned separately about an alleged robbery. After lengthy questioning the police are convinced that you both did the robbery. However they do not have evidence to get a conviction. In order to get one they will offer each of you the following deal.

If you admit to the robbery and testify against your friend, your friend will get 10 years in jail and you will go free.

If you both confess you both will get 5 years.

If neither confesses you would both get 1 year in jail for carrying a knife?

Although you and your friend are aware that you have both been offered the same deal, you are kept in separate cells so you do not know what either is planning to do. Given this scenario what would you do? What do you think your best friend will do? Which option would you choose and why? Ask yourself what thinking was behind your choice? Were you conscious of your thought process that led to your choice?

Chapter Three

A MODEL OF THOUGHT

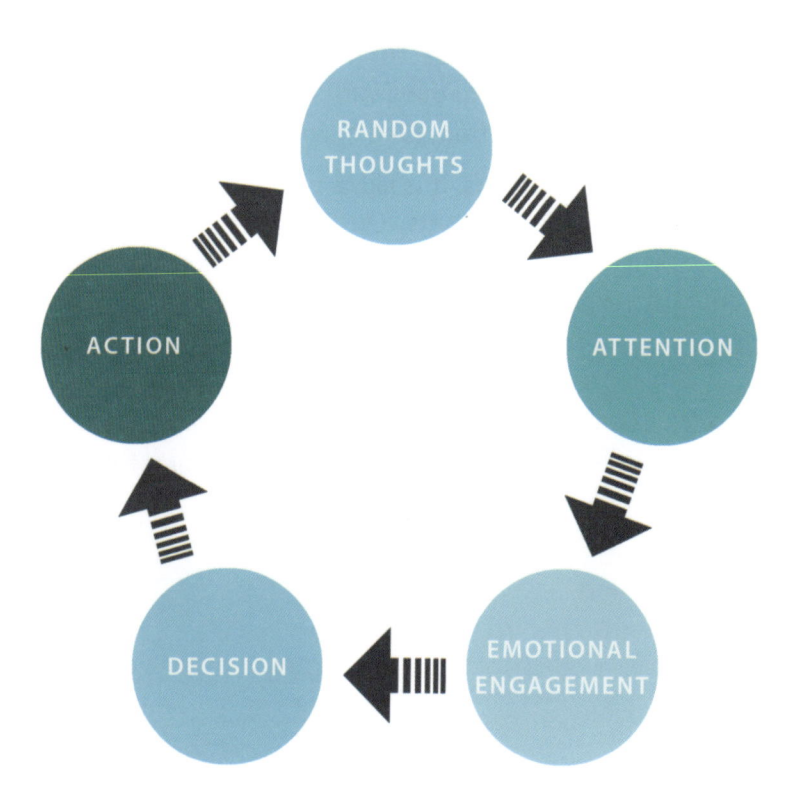

RANDOM THOUGHTS → ATTENTION → EMOTIONAL ENGAGEMENT → DECISION → ACTION → (back to RANDOM THOUGHTS)

Chapter Four
STEP ONE – RANDOM THOUGHTS

"Our achievements of today are the sum total of our thoughts of yesterday."

— *Pascal*

In the following section I set out the basis of the thinking process. For simplicity I have tried to describe thinking as a number of basic stages, beginning with random thoughts leading to a decision and then action. (See diagram)

The mind constantly thinks. It is like a television that is on all of the time with many channels. Out of this constant flow of thought emerge all of our experiences of life. Even asleep this flow continues in the form of dreams.

Thinking is a given, but what we choose to do with this flow of thought is down to us. We tend to see the result of our thinking and not the thinking process. How we engage with our minds is one of the key struggles to become fully human and fully alive.

STEP TWO – ATTENTION

"Children grow to fill the space we create for them."
— *Rabbi Andrew Sachs*

The majority of our thoughts come and go. They are of little significance. They appear and disappear just like clouds in the sky. It is only when we focus on a thought that it can become significant.

No matter how busy our minds are we can only hold one thought. A simple example of this is your breathing. Now that I have mentioned it your attention has switched to it. Advertisers know this well. They are experts at interfering with our random thinking process and grabbing our attention. That is why they use beautiful girls, stunning locations, bright colours and great soundtracks. They attack our senses to get our attention. And they have to do this quickly.

All advertisements are primarily about getting our attention. In the alcohol industry there is the concept of the three second rule. Insiders say that you get three seconds to make up your mind what you want to drink when you are asked in a bar.

In order to recognise the influences on our thinking and why we have the thoughts we do, we need to become aware of where our attention is. What is it that is currently grabbing our attention?

In modern life marketing is so pervasive by the time children are aged two their brand loyalties are already established. Below is an extract from the New York Times about how pervasive marketing can be.

> *The Walt Disney Company has started an ambitious and risky march towards the one corner of childhood it does*

not already dominate: newborns. Late last month, the company began pressing its newest priority, Disney Baby in 580 maternity hospitals in the US. More than 200,000 bodysuits will be given away free. They will then go on sale on Amazon for $9.99. "To get that mom thinking about her family's first park experience before her first child is even born is a home run," said a Disney spokesman.

Disney is not the only company that is spending millions getting parents' and children's attention and trying to control their thinking. Just look how many young children now have mobile phones.

We are all aware of the huge endorsements that sports stars get. The reason businesses are so willing to pay such huge amounts is that the sports star gets attention.

This type of influence was recognised 50 years ago by Eric Fromm in his book *To Have or to Be* when he claimed – 'Society has to solve a difficult problem, how to break a persons' will without them being aware of it. Yet by a complicated process of indoctrination, rewards, punishment, a fitting ideology, it solves this problem so well that most people believe they are following their own will and are unaware that they are being manipulated.'

Look at the brand loyalty for example to Apple, Manchester United, and Nike. Look at the intense rivalry between opposing fans of two different football brands. Fans will queue up at midnight for the latest game release or mobile phone. Consider the extreme phenomena of the suicide bombers where young people are willing to sacrifice themselves for a piece of thinking.

STEP THREE – EMOTIONAL ENGAGEMENT

"If cancer hadn't nearly killed me, I'd be just another selfish celebrity egomaniac. The most important thing I learned from the illness was setting aside my rock star ego and concentrating on what really matters. I have nearly died – and have seen what is real. It is nothing to do with money. So I have started to get to know people in the village where I live for the first time. I walk around and have cups of tea with the lady opposite – there never seemed to be time to do that before. Most of all I have learned to be happy. And I am happiest just being at home. "

– Chris Rea

It is not enough to grab our attention. Something else is required: emotional engagement. To stay with a thought it has to emotionally engage us. It may trigger a happy emotion, a sense of fear, or a feeling of hunger etc.

We all have unique preferences. In fact we all have an enormous list of things that can have a special meaning to us. At the top of everyone's list is one's own name.

We can be in a room full of people engrossed in conversation but if we hear our name spoken across the room our attention will immediately switch. In the case of a new mother the slightest murmur from her baby will immediately grab her attention.

The marketing people grab our attention and then try to get us to emotionally engage with their product. They create slogans like McDonalds' - 'Happy Meals' and BMW's - 'Joy comes in 3's. They use the full range of emotions from fear to joy to ensure we engage with their message. Slogans like Nike's – 'Just Do It' may suggest little intellectual or qualitative thinking.

After a thought has emotionally engaged us, we have to choose how to deal with those emotions. Often the choice is to do nothing. We get distracted and move onto something else. If we think about food often we have to eat to resolve those emotions. Much of our eating habits are linked to our emotional states. Comfort eating is an example of people using food to placate their emotions.

STEP FOUR – DECISION

"Even the simplest act is the culmination of a vast amount of neural activity unfolding below the level of our awareness. What you are aware of is the decision but you are not aware of the process that led to the decision."

– Francis Crick

Our emotional states play a significant role in the choices and decisions we make. Often it can be easier to do something, anything, rather than be still, sit with our emotional discontent and reflect on the underlying causes. A study from neuroscientist Laine Young suggests that our ability to make proper decisions is located in the region of the brain that regulates emotions. If we lose touch with our emotions we lose the ability to function effectively as human beings because we become unable to deal with choices and make decisions.

We spend money emotionally. Often if our spending is out of control it is a sign of an underlying emotional imbalance. The world of marketing tries to sell us something to remedy this imbalance but it is often just a temporary fix.

Often pervasive marketing has helped to create the emotional imbalance. Take a close look at your finances and if you are overdrawn all over the place then maybe you are emotionally all over the place too. The next major decisions you make try to understand and recognise the emotion that motivated you to act in a particular way or make a specific choice.

STEP FIVE – ACTION

At the action stage we are doing something to address a perceived need. Every day we have lots of individual thoughts but most of them we never act upon. The thoughts just come and go. One day a thought will force us into action whilst on another day it will not. All activity in life is the result of the decision to act out a thought.

Take a close look at someone's actions and it will reveal the quality of their thinking. Take a close look at your own behaviour and it will be a great mirror to the quality of your own thinking. Being flexible in our thinking and being willing to change our minds is a skill we should nourish and develop. If you are heading down the wrong road in life one of the best things you can do is stop to reflect on the thinking that brought you here.

The next time you make a decision recognise how you possibly became emotionally engaged with a random thought and then came to a decision to act on that emotion.

Chapter Five
BARRIERS TO THINKING

A farmer's horse ran away one day and all the villagers came to him saying, "O what bad luck you have had. Your horse that you need to do your work is gone!" The farmer shrugged his shoulders and said "Who knows good luck bad luck!" Several days later, the farmer's horse returned, followed by a herd of wild horses!

"Oh what good luck you have had!" said the villagers. The farmer shrugged his shoulders and said "Who knows good luck bad luck!" The farmer's son whilst trying to ride one of the wild horses fell off and broke his leg. The villagers again suggested that this was bad luck whilst the farmer's response was the same.

Soon afterwards an army came through the village and took all the young men to fight in the war but could not take the injured farmer's son. The Villager's response was "O what good luck you have had." The farmer shrugged his shoulders and said "Who knows good luck bad luck!"

I am sure we have all had events in life that we labelled good luck or bad luck only to find later that these assumptions were wrong.

Labelling our lives can be a dangerous occupation! Every thought we have helps build neural networks and affects our brain's chemistry. Thinking changes the thinker. Go about in a rage and the brain will generate the chemical associated with the state of rage.

Being angry, holding onto grudges, failing to forgive long term will eventually damage our health. Research has shown that as little as five minutes in meditation can alter the chemical balance of the brain. What then is ten years of holding onto a grudge capable of?

It is clear that actions have consequences but it is also true that emotions and emotional states have consequences. Medical research into drug trials and medical procedures has shown that there is a strong correlation between outcomes and the level of optimism that the patient has about a particular treatment. A new drug tends to work better than an old drug even if only from a placebo effect. A key indicator for the success of intervention with patients is the quality of their thinking before they begin the treatment.

Stress, our environment, lack of sleep, the food we eat, and trauma all affects the chemical make-up of our brains. Suffer long term stress and the brain's chemical make-up can be adversely affected, impairing our ability to function effectively. Andrew Willoughby in his book 'Protecting Children From Depression' states that 'The brain only keeps a small amount of these essential neurotransmitters and makes new ones whilst we sleep. Working long hours, stress, or lack of sleep can exhaust the brain's supply of these important neurotransmitters.'

So it is essential that we take care with our thoughts because they do have a major impact on our physical and psychological health. What we think not only influences how we interpret our lives it also is a key factor in the quality of our lives. Have you ever sat down and taken time to recognise and name the thoughts that are holding you back from living the life you dreamed of?

Chapter Six
PAST EXPERIENCES AND KNOWLEDGE

There is the story of a couple on holiday in London. One night they went to the theatre to see the murder mystery, *The Mousetrap*. They took a taxi to the theatre. Paying the fair they did not give the driver a tip. As the taxi pulled off the driver shouted who did it!

The Mousetrap is a play by Agatha Christie that has been running in the West End for more than 30 years. It is a tradition of the cast to ask the audience at the end not to reveal who the murderer was in order not to spoil the show for future audiences.

How we experience the world is influenced by the experiences we have already had and the information we hold. Research carried in by the Behavioural Economist Dan Ariley has demonstrated how external events and information influence our perception of reality. He took two groups of students. He gave one of them a list of words associated with youthfulness and the other words associated with old age.

Both groups had to make up sentences using the words. On completion of the exercise they were later observed walking across the campus. The groups who used the words associated with old age walked much slower than the other group.

What we see when we look out at the world is affected by what we have just seen. Our perception of colour changes dependant on what colour we have just seen. Sound also affects our mood. Play loud rock music in the car and we are likely to find ourselves speeding. The people we spend time with have an impact on our quality of thinking. Spend time with optimistic upbeat people and you have a good chance of becoming more optimistic.

In the first Gulf War the US army had great difficulty in getting their soldiers to eat enough calories whilst in combat zones. The soldiers complained about the quality of the food. The army reworked the menu and upped the quality of the ingredients. This made no difference. As part of research to try and find out why this was the case they then took groups of soldiers and served them the same food in three different restaurants. The better the decor of the restaurant's the better they rated the food. They discovered that the environment we have an experience in has an impact on our perception of that experience.

The environment that surrounds us has also an impact on the quality of our thinking. Being aware of this will help change the quality of our thinking. Think for a moment about the level of enthusiasm and thinking style that we all bring to our two week vacation every year. Why do we often choose to leave that enthusiasm and thinking style at the airport when we return home?

Chapter Seven
THE ROLE OF THE EGO

"It isn't easy to do. But it's essential to a happy life. I have seen marriages fail, friends become estranged, and whole communities divided all because neither side was prepared to say: I got it wrong. Forgive me."

– *Chief Rabbi Sachs*

Our emotional states play a significant role in the choices and decisions we make. A Lord Chief Justice in the UK once said that if charged with a parking offence for which he had to attend court he would hire a solicitor to defend him in court. The reason he gave was that no one can be objective about them self. What he was intimating was that our egos get in the way of seeing ourselves as we are and reality for what it is.

The ego has been described as the inflated part of ourselves that likes to be in control and feel superior to others. It is our false self. Our ego likes to take centre stage and do our thinking for us.

In the movie *The Aviator* there was a great line said to Howard Hughes. It was: "You know what the problem is with you Howard Hughes? There is too much Howard Hughes in Howard Hughes."

The ego is the doer. It manages and directs the person. It creates the identity and constructs the mask we wear to allow us to function in the world. The ego can be one of our most cunning adversaries. How many people would be happy to openly admit that they have a big ego or that it was their ego that was running things? A way to check if your ego is to the forefront is to ask yourself do you ever admit to being wrong or apologise for your mistakes.

If our ego is the dominant part of our personality then it will have a negative impact on the quality of our thinking. Trying to rebalance the situation will result in the ego struggling to prevent us succeeding. So realise that you have an ego and take care to keep it in check otherwise it will control your thinking and want to keep you on the treadmill of ambition and self-centredness.

Chapter Eight
RECOGNISING THE NEED TO CHANGE

A great king called all his wise men together and asked them to make him something that when he was happy and looked at it, it would make him sad and when he was sad if he looked at it, it would make him happy. After many years, and lots of debate they returned with a gold ring for him to wear.

The king asked how the ring would make him happy when he was sad and sad when he was happy. The wise men said that inside the ring was an engraved message which read – EVEN THIS WILL PASS!

A major barrier to improving the quality of our thinking is that we do not see any need to change! If our thinking has worked well up to now we may assume that it will continue to work just as well in the future. After all you probably have not given much thought to your own process of thinking. Up to now you may have had a successful life.

As Tony De Mello intimated in his book *Awareness*, we may in fact have got through our life up to now 'asleep'. We may be very comfortable where we are in life and feel no need to change.

Collectively as a society and individually we experience this illusion on a regular basis. We can see this on a micro scale when someone is brutally murdered in a small community. Often neighbours are interviewed and are shocked that such a thing could happen in their local area.

De Mello suggests that a good question to ask yourself to see if you are awake or not is: does anything shock or surprise you? Many of the mystics have said that until we accept that everyone is capable of everything we are asleep.

It may be difficult to accept but we need to realise that, given the right set of circumstances, we are all capable of everything. Philip Zimbardo in his book *The Lucifer Effect* illustrates this reality. He was part of the defence team for one of the soldiers accused of cruelty at Abu Ghraib Prison during the Iraq war. He argued that it was the environment that influenced the soldiers' actions. What happened was not a case of a few rotten apples but good people being put in an environment that was 'a rotten barrel'.

Ask yourself how is your thinking serving you? Have you found contentment? Is your thinking helping to create or solve life's challenges?

Chapter Nine
THINKING DESIGN FAULTS

A woman waiting at an airport for her delayed flight bought a book, a coffee and packet of cookies to pass the time. She was deep in her book when suddenly she realised that there was a young man sitting next to her. He stretched out his hand and ate cookie from the packet of cookies lying between them. Not wanting to make a fuss the woman said nothing and continued eating from the packet of cookies. However she began to become angry as the young man continued to help himself to her cookies. Every time she ate a biscuit he ate one too.

When there was only one left the young man lifted it broke it in two and offered her half. She took half and thought, 'what an insolent man! How uneducated! He didn't even thank me!' She had never met someone so arrogant and was relieved when her flight was called. She grabbed her bags and went off towards the boarding gate.

After boarding the plane she reached into her bag for her book. She was shocked to find her packet of cookies unopened. If my packet of cookies are here she thought, feeling terrible, that other packet of cookies was his and he tried to share it with me. Too late to apologise she realised it was her who was uneducated, insolent and had rushed to judgement.

How many times in our lives have we known for certain that something happened in a particular way, only to discover later that it wasn't true? How many times has our thinking raced to the wrong conclusions?

Being able to make fast decisions is often a useful skill. Ten thousand years ago we needed to be able to work out quickly if a pattern in the distance was a tiger. However this quick decision process is not always best applied to modern life. Being able to take the time and reflect on information in front of us can sometimes be much more useful.

Professor V.S. Ramachandran of the University of California suggests that our brains process information through two distinct paths. One path goes through consciousness whilst another bypasses our consciousness. An example would be driving a car. Did you ever drive somewhere and only realise after you arrived that you had little or no memory of the journey.

You can drive a car and hold a conversation with one of the passengers. Our conscious thought is on the conversation whilst another part of our brain is engaged in driving the car. He argues we cannot do the reverse.

Therefore we can do things but this does not mean that we are giving our full attention to them. If we take this to the extreme, we can actually be living our lives without being fully present to them. Paying attention to every day situations, being present to the now and learning to reflect and come to a measured decision is a skill that if developed will improve the quality of your thinking and decision making.

Chapter Ten
THINKING IN STORY MODE

A Japanese tourist was walking around the National Museum in Dublin and stopped at the dinosaur skeleton. There was no indication of the age of the exhibit so he asked the museum attendant how old it was. The attendant replied "The dinosaur is five million years and nine months old." Surprised at this answer the tourist asked the attendant "How can you be so accurate?" The attendant replied "I started working here nine months ago and it was five million years old then."

This little story describes how our brains on automatic pilot can arrive at conclusions and interpret facts in a simplistic fashion. Our brains are designed to look for links and come up with simple solutions.

When something happens to us we want to know why? But we can sometimes fail to realise that the desire for a simple answer can cause us to miss the point. For example, suppose one morning you are walking down the street of your local town and in the distance you see someone lying on the footpath at the bottom of a ladder.

What do you think just happened? The fact that we have very little actual information does not prevent our brains from constructing a story. It takes a lot of effort to catch ourselves doing this and prevent the brain from its automatic story mode.

If we have three pieces of information A, B and C the brain likes to think of a story that connects the three, even if there is no connection. Stories and connections are easy to remember and that is one reason why the brain links events even if there are no links there.

Here are some of the different conclusions that might be reached on seeing the man lying at the bottom of the ladder:-

The man fell off the ladder.

The man was walking down the street whilst texting on his phone, walked into the ladder and knocked himself out.

The man was crossing the road and was involved in a hit and run accident and just happened to be knocked to the ground beside the ladder.

The man was walking down the street and took sick and fainted beside the ladder.

The man is a friend of yours and saw you walking in the distance. He decided to play a prank on you and lie down beside the ladder.

The man was murdered. Someone threw him off the roof and left the ladder there to make it look like and accident.

Which of the above scenarios did you think of if any? It can often take much less effort to arrive at an incorrect answer than to take the time to look at various options. Did you conclude that you didn't know what happened and it would be incorrect to arrive at any assumptions? To think better we need to become more comfortable with not knowing, with staying with the question.

Making assumptions too early in the thinking process can force us to manipulate facts so that they fit into our assumptions and thus ignore facts that would force us to change the story. Skilled people know this. Detectives who work on murder cases try to compensate for this potential error. What they often do is not reveal one vital piece of evidence that only they and the murderer know. This is because they can use this to confirm they have got the person for the crime.

The next time we find ourselves jumping to conclusions we may need to take a step back and see what we actually know. Be aware of taking an over-simplistic view of things. A fact is a verified piece of information. Ask yourself could you prove in a court of law what you think is true?

When trying to make sure your thinking is correct make sure to also look out for facts that may prove your opinion wrong. Doing this will help you gain a better grasp of your interpretation of reality. It may also prevent unnecessary anxiety or stress for you and others.

Chapter Eleven
SURPRISING THOUGHTS

A tourist was driving through the Irish countryside in his hire car when the car suddenly stopped. Unsure of what to do he tried phoning for help but was in an area where there was no mobile phone signal. He got out of the car and looked in at the engine. Everything looked ok. He was perplexed. Suddenly he heard a voice saying, "It's your spark plugs. You need to take your spark plugs out and clean them." Looking around to see where the voice was coming from he could see no one except a horse staring over the hedge at him. Surprised he ignored the horse and went back to looking at the engine. He heard the voice again, "It's your spark plugs. You need to take your spark plugs out and clean them."

The tourist looked around and realised it was the horse who was talking to him. Not knowing what to do, he decided to take the horse's advice. He took the spark plugs out, cleaned them, put them back in and the car started.

In a state of shock he drove off. After a while he was passing by a pub and decided to stop and go in for a drink to steady his nerves. The barman noticed that the man was agitated and asked him what was up. The tourist told the story about the hire car and the horse. On hearing the story the barman asked the man "Was that a black horse or a brown horse that gave you the advice." The tourist answered "It was a brown horse." The barman replied, "You are a very lucky man as that black horse knows nothing about cars."

When someone starts to tell a joke, although we do not realise it, we become tense. Simple jokes like, 'a man walks into a bar' immediately creates tension because subconsciously we know that some bars can be threatening places. We do not know where the bar is, we do not know if the man is a stranger in the bar, or if he is alone? This all adds to a feeling of tension.

All these questions in our subconscious means the adrenalin begins to flow. The best jokes are the ones that create the highest amount of tension for the longest time. That is one reason why the comedian Billy Connolly is a successful comedian. He begins a story, creates tension and then goes off on several tangents, often for a considerable amount of time.

This all creates tension in the audience and it is only sometime later that he delivers the punch-line and releases the tension.

A joke is a story that creates tension. The punch-line is the release mechanism for that tension. Laughing and shaking with laughter is the body's way of getting rid of the tension. But why write about jokes in a book about thinking? Lonergan, the Canadian Jesuit in his book 'Insight' describes getting insights to life as a similar process to getting the punchline in a joke. He describes the human condition as 'the unrestricted desire to know' and uses the example of a detective story: 'in the ideal detective story the reader is given all the clues but fails to spot the criminal.' What he is describing is the process of developing our understanding of life, of getting new insights. Lonergan goes on to warn us that unless we realise this desire is a natural part of the human condition it can lead to feelings of incompleteness and disaffection.

As humans we have a need to know. This need provides us with much of our drive in life. We are naturally inquisitive. Spend a day with a three year old and you will know all about this. We ask questions. We reflect on our life and try to make sense of it. Humour has the ability to lighten the heart and release tension.

It also has the ability to provide us with useful insights into how we perceive the world and can be a vehicle to drive us to change for the better.

Laughter is good for your physical and mental health. Being able to laugh at ourselves stops us from becoming too serious. It ensures that our thinking about life does not become stuck. The one thing about jokes is that once you get the punch-line you cannot 'un-get' it. Insights are the same. Once you get a new insight into life you cannot go back to believing what you believed before. The process of growing and gaining new insights begins all over again.

If you are puzzled by a particular situation in life maybe changing how you think about it may reveal the punchline. Viktor E. Frankl, who survived the Concentration Camps during the Second World War, later wrote, 'The attempt to develop a sense of humour and to see things in a humorous light is some kind of a trick learned while mastering the art of living.'

Chapter Twelve
THINKING ABOUT TIME

A farmer had four pigs to sell at the local market. He had no trailer so he put a pig in his wheel barrow and pushed it down the road several miles to the market. He went back home, put another pig in the wheel barrow and did the same. His neighbour was watching him and after he had taken all four pigs to the market and sold them the neighbour enquired why he didn't borrow his trailer and take all the pigs to the market at once, because what he was doing was an awful waste of time. "Sure what's time to a pig?" the farmer replied.

Time is the one great leveller. Whether we are the President of America, the CEO of a multinational or the postman, we all get only 24 hours each day. We spend our time, one day at a time and once spent it is gone forever. There is no bank where we can deposit our time for future use. Someone once said that all activity in life is just humans trying to manipulate time.

If you are engrossed in your favourite hobby you will wonder where the time went. Get delayed at an airport on your way home from a vacation and time will drag. Our ability to judge time alters as we age. When we are young a day can last forever but as we get old even a year seems to fly.

There is a story where the grim reaper appeared to the rich man to claim his life. Not wanting to die the rich man tried to cut a deal. The grim reaper came up with the choice, "Your money or your life." The man thought about the offer for a while and replied "You may take my life as I need my money for my old age."

One of the greatest disappointments when we grow old can be the feeling of the unlived life. We can waste our precious time and fail to live the life we dreamt we could. This can happen because somewhere along the way we begin to look outside ourselves for contentment. We search for the approval of others; we live our life according to others' expectations; we fail to follow our own desires and forget what we are passionate about. This frenetic activity of trying to fit into some preconceived notion of ourselves can take us further and further away from our true selves to a lonely and desolate place. It can be a place where we apparently have it all and need more!

When we turn up on Planet Earth, we carry no 'baggage'. Growing up, the development of our ego, peer pressure, criticism, poor parenting, bullying and the absence of proper socialisation can damage us. Suddenly we realise we have become stressed with all the demands we place on our time.

If you find yourself multitasking, trying to be all things to all people, or having difficulty saying no, it is likely that you are trying too hard to be someone you were never meant to be. It is also likely that you are spending your precious time on the things in life that are not meeting your deepest needs.

Eric Fromm in the early 1970s predicted the rise of consumerism and retail therapy long before it took hold. He says that people have forgotten how to be and have chosen to have instead. Society can judge people by what they have, not who they are. Celebrity and reality television is a clear example of this. People want success, fame and recognition without the effort. Celebrities become famous for being famous.

The good news is that you do not have to go on an epic journey, slay a dragon, marry prince charming or rescue a princess to come home to yourself.

All you have to do is relax, slow down and begin to pay attention to your life.

Ask yourself; when you are on your own do you like the person you are with? Would we as children like spending a day with the adult we have become? Have we lost our sense of adventure? Have we forgotten our sense of fun? Have we become old before our time? Are we strolling down the path of personal growth or running on the treadmill of life?

Chapter Thirteen
THINKING ABOUT WORK

*'When all the trees have been cut down, when all the animals
have been hunted, when all the waters are polluted,
when all the air is unsafe to breathe,
only then will you discover that you cannot eat money.'*
— *American Indian Prophecy*

A business consultant on holiday sitting on a beach, to pass the time, began to watch the local fisherman going about his work. He observed that the fisherman went out in his boat every morning and returned a few hours later with some fish. He sold the fish from his boat and stopped work around midday. It appeared that he earned just enough money to feed his wife and family. The rest of the day he sat on the beach, played with his children, talked to his friends, drank wine and watching the world go by.

The consultant after analysing his week of observation recommended to the fisherman a new business model. If the fisherman worked full time he could earn enough money to buy a bigger boat. He could then employ a crew and catch enough fish to buy a second boat. If they all worked long hours they could make enough money to build a fish processing factory and begin to export the fish and get a better price. If he did this for 20 years he could make enough money then he could work part time. He could then relax and spend time on the beach with his family and friends drinking wine.

What we think about work often has a significant impact on how we live our lives. We all know the person in work who thinks they are indispensable. They work long hours, take work home and get their e-mails 24/7. Just watch how many business people reach for the mobile the minute the aeroplane touches down.

What does this ceaseless preoccupation with work do to the quality of our thinking? When do we get the opportunity to be alone with our thoughts? If you are working more than 40 hours per week, (and it is not because you are on the minimum wage) why? What are you working for? What is it you are avoiding? Whom are you neglecting?

An article published on the BBC news website by Andrew Bomford claimed that inhabitants of a small Greek Island live on average 10 years longer than people in the rest of Europe. One of the residents asked what it was that made them live so long claimed it was the wine. He makes around 700 litres of wine a year from his own vineyard. When asked did he drink it all himself he remarked: "No, I drink it with my friends."

He had been diagnosed with terminal cancer and given nine months to live in America. Returning home to die he began to meet with his friends and drink wine. "I found my friends in the village where I was born, and we started drinking. I thought at least I'll die happy. Everyday we got together and we drank wine and I waited. As time went by I felt stronger. Forty five years later I am still here. A while ago I went back to the US and tried to find my doctors. They are all dead."

Researchers on the island believe other factors lead to the longevity of the island inhabitants where the rates of smoking are relatively low, midday naps are the norm, the pace of life is slow and people socialise frequently with family and friends. How much different does that sound to our current lifestyles?

Chapter Fourteen
THINKING ABOUT POSSESSIONS

Two brothers lived on a farm and operated a business as vegetable merchants. They travelled around the country buying produce from local farmers and re-selling it again. Both were bachelors. Their parents had left them the farm and business when they both died over 10 years before.

The older brother was industrious and hard working whilst the younger liked the easy life regularly socialising and drinking to the wee hours.

One evening the older brother asked the younger one to ensure that he got up early the next morning to take a load of potatoes to market and that he was not to be going out drinking.

The next evening the older brother returned home to find the younger brother had gone to the pub got drunk and had not done any work. This threw the older brother into a temper and he said: "Ever since our parents died I have been working my fingers to the bone 12 hours a day, six days a week trying to keep the business together and a roof over our heads and you have been out drinking, partying and enjoying yourself." To this the younger brother replied, "Well you have no-one to blame only yourself!"

Now I am not suggesting we abdicate our responsibilities, or that we all adopt hedonistic lifestyles. I just want you to consider if we keep thinking the way we do then what quality of life does that give us? If we choose to be serious all the time, a workaholic, a professional worrier, then maybe we get the life we deserve. Are we working for a living or living to work? Are you working to buy a bigger house so that you have more room to store all of the stuff that you have now acquired?

Many modern jobs require us to stare at a computer screen 40 hours a week, the only difference being what is on the screen? Is what's on your screen how you define you? Is all the stuff you feel you need to acquire and hold onto worth spending the best part of your life staring at that screen?

Every thought we have results in a chemical reaction and alters our brain activity and make up. Studies on people's brains have shown that shopping causes the production of dopamine in our brains, a chemical that is associated with happiness. Dr Gregory Burns from Edinburgh University suggests that this is one of the reasons why some people can buy shoes they never wear.

Take a good look at the stuff you have accumulated on your trip to this planet. What does that say about the quality of your thinking about possessions?

Chapter Fifteen
THINKING ABOUT FRIENDSHIP

"A friend isn't someone who's just always there for you. It's someone who understands you a bit more than you understand yourself."
— Ihanababy

Once upon a time a man was discontent with his life. A friend seeing his discontentment gave him a book to read. This book was a great help and in it there were recommendations for other books. He bought all of the other books and read them.

A couple of years later the two friends met up again. The one who had recommended the first book asked his friend how he was doing. He replied that he was doing much better and had gained some great insights from all the reading he had done. He had read over 500 books in his search for enlightenment. His friend said it was great to see him becoming so enlightened but asked was he still discontent? The friend replied, "Yes, it's my job!"

Often in life we can distract ourselves with almost anything in order to face up to the difficult choices we know we need to make. In these types of situations good friends can if we listen carefully challenge us to see life how it actually is. They will often question our assumptions and steer us in the right direction. Our true friends also allow us to get a glimpse of how others see us and how they see the world. They can provide us with another window on the world.

Our friends are also here to recognise, guide and support us. Good friends reflect us back to ourselves. They should challenge us to be the best we can be. It is therefore necessary for us to nourish a circle of friends whom we respect, admire and can share great conversation with. A good place to start to develop new friends would be a local reading group, or why not take up a new sport that involves joining a club. Making new friends will give us a new perspective on the quality of our own thinking, our belief systems and life.

Chapter Sixteen
WHAT THINKING FRAMES YOUR LIFE?

"Most people would rather die than think, in fact they do."
—Bertrand Russell

An old farmer in ancient China owed a debt to the local warlord. Due to the poor winter and bad harvest he was unable to repay the debt. However he had a beautiful daughter whom the warlord wished to marry, but she despised the warlord. In order to settle the debt the warlord came up with a proposal. He would place two pebbles in a bag, one white and one black. The farmer's daughter would then pick one pebble out of the bag. If the pebble was black then she would have to marry the warlord and if white she could go free.

When the farmer's daughter heard the proposal she was horrified as she knew the warlord was dishonest and would rig the bet by placing two black pebbles in the bag. However she decided she had no choice and that she would take on the bet to protect her father.

She put her hand into the bag and picked out a pebble and without letting anyone see it she dropped it onto the road that was full of different coloured pebbles. She apologised for her clumsy mistake and said that she could tell what colour of pebble she had dropped by looking in the bag. If the pebble was black then she must have dropped a white pebble. She picked the pebble out of the bag. It was black and so she won her freedom.

We cannot all be as ingenious as the farmer's daughter when faced with dilemmas in life. Often we do not have the knowledge or expertise to fully understand risk and make properly informed choices. In these occasions we use mental shortcuts known as heuristics. They allow us to make informed guesses. But many of us don't properly understand probability or risk and this can lead to mistakes and poor choices.

Professional poker players have to be sharp thinkers. Here is an example of the type of thinking they do. Their thinking about a hand of cards ranges across all these possibilities.

How good a hand do I have?

How good a hand do my opponents have?

How good a hand do my opponents think I have?

How good a hand do my opponents think that I think I have?

How good a hand do my opponents think that I think they think I have?

When we reach stage five of thinking then it is nothing to do with what cards each player actually has.

Life, playing the hand we are dealt, can be similar to the poker player. We can be at stage one and concentrate only on the hand dealt and become dissatisfied because others appear to have been dealt a better hand. The creative people in life operate at level five. They pay little attention to what cards they or others have. They have a strategy for life and no matter what happens they concentrate on the task at hand.

Unfortunately, due to inappropriate thinking habits many of us never realise our full potential. We settle for less. One of the greatest tragedies of life is not that we all die but not all of us live fully. In conversation people often make you aware of their limitations. These are often nothing more than the result of their thinking. They have set artificial boundaries around themselves and their lives. If you think you are wrong you are right and if you think you are right you are right.

Much of life's adventure is realising that we are all capable of greatness. It is about discovering and developing our own special talent. Failing at something is much more rewarding that never having tried. Change your thinking. Do something, anything! Go on surprise yourself. Take up that hobby or go on that adventure you always promised yourself. Wouldn't it be a terrible tragedy to wait billions of years to come here and not let go of your comfort blanket and take a few risks somewhere along the way. Opportunity doesn't do home calls. The worst thing that can happen is you will end up dead and that is a given. Take a risk. We get motivated not by thinking about doing, we start something and the motivation follows. Now is the only time you have!

Chapter Seventeen
THINKING ABOUT WHAT YOU WANT

A little girl walked into a fruit shop with a banana peel in her hand. "What do you want?" said the shop assistant. The little girl replied "A refill please."

If you asked people what they wanted out of life their answers would be what they think would make them happy. We are built for happiness. You are probably chasing what you think will make you happy. Philosophers have written great volumes on the subject of happiness and what constitutes a worthwhile life. You may not have studied philosophy but we all develop our own philosophy of life.

I would suggest that we are all looking for something slightly different to happiness. What we all seek is joy. Imagine spending 70 years on this planet and never experiencing joy! Take a moment and recall the last time you felt some real joy. The world experienced collective joy in 2010 when 33 Chilean miners were rescued after being trapped over 1000 feet below ground for more than 60 days.

Children know about joy. What they do naturally is bring joy into everything they do. Before they become too self conscious they bring joy to all their activities by devoting their undivided attention to what they are doing.

As adults we can forget life is about joy and not about the car we drive, the job, the bank balance, our address or the house we live in. Joy comes from forgetting ourselves and inhabiting the moment. It comes from throwing yourself wholeheartedly into something. It's about putting fun back into life. Joy begins by being grateful. It can be found all around us if we just look. It's in a summer morning, a winter snow shower or an amazing sunset.

Are you amazed by life? The fact that you are here and witnessing the whole thing going on! Willoughby suggests that "Joy stands in stark contrast to what is important. The urgent list of things that need done.... we don't see joy as urgent but it is... in the surrender to joy you learn that you are not your thoughts."

So how do we acquire this joy? Well its free, it's an attitude we adopt. It's a free gift we give to ourselves. Begin by acting as if we already have this gift. Jump out of bed with a spring in your step. Greet the world each day with joy. Talk, walk, and act like a person full of joy.

Joy is a by product of humility. Stop taking yourself too seriously. Develop a sense of humour. Laugh at yourself. Smile. Believe in miracles. Expect the best. Let go of results and embrace uncertainty. It is only when we begin to get beyond our thinking, words, concepts and the analytical mind that we will begin to discover real joy. Marcel Marceau the great mime artist said: "The greatest moments in life leave us without words."

Joy is about forgetting the analysis and being in the moment. It is about taking the ego out of the equation. So go on risk building joy into your every day life. Forget about being all grown up and having to behave like a grown up. Give your ego a rest and go out and enjoy life again. Stop worrying about what others will think.

Joy is about your relationship with yourself. Imagine every day of the rest of your life with a person filled with joy – yourself. How much better would your life be if you became your own best friend instead of your own best critic? Imagine how better the people's lives that you come into contact with would be also. It is only in letting go of the illusion of control, about getting our false self out of the driving seat that we really begin to live.

This today, now, is all we have. Today is all there is. The fullness of life is available to us all right here, right now. Joy is a choice we make.

If you are using your intellect to placate your ego, to live up to some preconceived notion about how your life should be, to acquire more stuff, then don't be surprised if there is no end to the hunger. Don't be surprised is there is little or no joy in your life.

Everyday offers each of us a unique opportunity to learn and grow. All we have to do is show up with the right attitude and pay attention to what life offers us each day.

Most of the lessons we learn in life we have to experience for ourselves. Friends can point us in a direction but no other can do the work for us. No one can take a single step on the journey to awareness and self knowledge.

Yes we will make lots of mistakes. Like learning to ride a bicycle we all have to fall off many times before we find our own sense of balance and the courage to steer our own course.

The second half of this book sets out a programme of activities to assist you to improve the quality of your thinking and help you find a sense of balance and joy in your life.

PART TWO

Chapter Eighteen
THINKING ABOUT THE PAST

The past is the building blocks of each of our presents. Today's life is built on the foundations we have put in place every day up until now. Part of growing and developing as a person is the ability to reflect on the thoughts and decisions we have made in the past. In order to improve how we think about the past I suggest we need to adopt a no-blame ethos? Take responsibility for the past and stop apportioning blame!

As we go through life we gain more experience and hopefully become more astute. Reflecting on the past allows us to understand better what helped influence the path we have taken. However many of the choices we made in the past cannot be undone. Even something as simple as drinking a glass of water cannot be undone. All we can do with the past is change how we think about it.

The alternative is to hold on to regret. Doing this can drain our enthusiasm for today. When we hold onto regret we are simply using the benefit of hindsight to criticise ourselves. Regret keeps us a prisoner of our past. We take on the role of prisoner and jailer. Forgiveness is what we need. But often forgiving ourselves can be more difficult than forgiving others.

If we have regrets about how others have behaved towards us in the past we need to realise that in order to live a good life we have to take responsibilities for ourselves and our thoughts. We are responsible not only for what or how we think but also how we react to and deal with our life experiences. Blaming people for not treating you how you think they should have is as crazy as blaming the weather for how you feel. The weather is the weather. People are people. It is our thinking about the weather that causes the problem not the weather. And often it is our false expectations of others that cause us anguish.

Understand that people often act out of self-interest. If given the choice, people will often put themselves ahead of us. That's what we all do most of the time. People have weaknesses and driven by self interest will act out of those weaknesses. Often they have no idea of how we think they should behave.

Dr Fred Luskin in his book *Forgive for Good* says that if we get our thinking wrong we can develop a victim mentality. He says that we do this by taking things too personally. We blame others for how we feel and develop a grievance story about what happened to us. We are responsible for how we feel no one else. If we have a victim mentality then it may be time to change how we think about the past in order to be able to successfully move on.

Chapter Nineteen
THINKING ABOUT THE PRESENT

On a cold January morning in Washington metro station a man took a violin out of its case and began to play. He played six Bach pieces for about 45 minutes. It was rush hour and thousands of people passed through the station in those 45 minutes, most on their way to work.

Three minutes went by and a middle-aged man noticed there was a musician playing. He slowed his pace and then hurried on to meet his schedule.

A minute later, the violinist received his first tip; a woman threw the money in the tin and without stopping walked by.

A few minutes later, a man leaned against the wall to listen but then looked at his watch and moved on.

The one who paid the most attention was a three-year-old boy. His mother tried to hurry him along but the kid stopped to look at the violinist. Finally his mother walked on dragging the kid behind her.

This was the same story with a few other children whose parents all tried to hurry them along.

In the 45 minutes the musician played, only six people stopped and delayed for a while. About twenty gave him money but didn't slow down. He got $32. When he stopped playing the silence took over. No one noticed. No one applauded, nor was there any recognition.

No one knew the violinist was Joshua Bell, one of world's best. He had just played some of the world's most difficult pieces on his $3.5m Stradivarius. *Interview* magazine said his playing 'does nothing less than tell human beings why they bother to live.' Two days earlier Joshua Bell had played a sold-out concert in Boston where the average seat price was $100.

This story is true. Joshua Bell playing incognito in the metro station was organised by the *Washington Post* as part of a social experiment about perception.

This experiment describes many of our life experiences. We can rush through life and fail to see that each day is unique. A day is all we have. It can offer us great possibilities if we just take the time to engage fully with each day.

One problem with approaching each day as unique is that we as humans like familiarity. Much of our energy can go into trying to ensure that today is just like yesterday. We like things as they are and fear change.

Are you the person who always parks in the same car park space? Are you the one who sits in the same seat in Church? Do you order the same thing from the menu?

We all have a difficult balancing act and that is each day to set a balance between the familiar and the risk of the new.

Everyday requires our attention. All great sports people know about paying attention. One key attribute they all share is the ability to focus their undivided attention on the present. To be a successful sportsperson you must learn to be in the moment. Every golfer knows the most important shot is the one they are about to play.

To live a content life we have to learn to be in the moment. As John Main the Benedictine monk said that we need to learn to die to the ego. We have to learn the balance between focus and flow. A good way of learning to be in the moment is meditation where the purpose is to still the mind and stay with the 'now'. Why not join a class or begin some private practice?

Chapter Twenty
THINKING ABOUT THE FUTURE

"A baby is God's opinion that the world should go on."
— Carl Sandburg

It never fails to amaze me just how loved new arrivals to planet earth are. After all each baby is a complete stranger. The conversations about whom they resemble. It is part of the ritualistic welcoming for the new arrival. But what is it that makes babies so loveable? In part it is their vulnerability. That is what attracts us to them.

One day we all arrived on this planet as strangers. We were unknown yet loved. We had done nothing to earn this love except turn up. Unfortunately this idea of it being enough to just be seems to fade as we mature. We can spend most of our adult lives trying to be accepted and loved, forgetting that it was our vulnerability that made us all lovable in the first place.

Eric Fromm the writer and philosopher said that many of us have forgotten how 'to be' and have chosen 'to have' as their mode of living. This can drive us to a life that becomes a series of accumulations and maintenance. The more we commit to the more maintenance we have to do. This is one reason why most middle aged people have no time to do anything new.

Does any of this sound familiar? Dealing with the future is about being open to change. The more one has preconceived ideas about how we or things should be, the harder one has to work to achieve this.

Realising that we have little or no control over the future can be a great release. It is the not knowing that helps us to remain motivated in life.

Dealing with what life sends us requires flexibility of thinking and a willingness to take risks with who we think we are.

John O'Donohue, the Irish Poet and scholar often talked about how one phone call with some news could change our lives for ever. The ground beneath our feet has shifted and there is no way of going back. It is in these situations that the quality of our thinking will be challenged. If we have not done the self examination, the critical analysis, we may be found wanting when the future brings unexpected challenges.

Chapter Twenty-one
SIX-DAY PROGRAMME OF DISCOVERY

In the next section I have set out a six-day programme of exercises to assist in improving the quality of your thinking and help you successfully meet any challenges the future may hold. It focuses on our five senses through which we experience life.

> *"Without sensory data it is difficult to live in reality.*
> *To get it we must give ourselves permission*
> *to look, listen, touch and explore the world."*
> *– John Bradshaw*

DAY 1 – COLOUR

During day one begin to look again at colour. The world is full of colour. The older we get the fewer colours we seem to notice in our lives. Go to any management meeting of senior executives and you will see a bunch of grey men in a grey world.

The great artists saw the world differently. They took time to look. One once said no matter what colour you paint the sky one day you will be right. On this first day get up early enough to watch the sunrise. Notice how light brings colour to life. Count how many different colours you can recognise in this day. How many different shades of green will you see today? Notice is your world one of pastels or bright vibrant colours. Psychologists know the role that colours play in influencing our moods and choices.

Forget looking at the cars, buildings, trees, fields and look at the variety of colours. Look to see the colours of shadows. Wear something bright for a change and see how it affects your mood and how people react to you. Look to see and recognise how the evening light and twilight sucks the colour out of the landscape, and how moonlight and the stars light the landscape. When is the last time you starred up at the sky or watched the full moon appear in the night sky?

DAY 2 – SOUND

The second day is about the sound of our lives. The soundtrack of our lives has an impact on how we feel and our emotional state. An example of this is when we go to the movies. Are you aware that most people go to the movies for the sounds not just the pictures? The director of *Slum Dog Millionaire* Danny Boyle has said that the soundtrack is 70% to 80% of the experience of any movie. Producers know this and that is why they hire the best composer and sound effects engineers to complement the film. If you compiled a list of the top movie soundtracks you would also be making a list of the biggest box office successes. *Star Wars, Titanic, The Godfather, Psycho, Dirty Dancing*, The Bond movies, etc. What would *Jaws* be without the haunting theme?

We fill our world with artificial sound each day. We switch on mobiles, MP3 players, radios and televisions and drown out the natural sound of life. On this day switch off the noise. When you awaken in the morning lie still and listen. What are the sounds you hear that are there each day but you have failed to notice?

If you take a shower in the morning listen to the sound of the water. Listen to the sound of the sink filling with water to brush your teeth or shave. Listen to the sound of the kettle boiling.

Notice the sound of your own footsteps. Hear the sound of the front door closing behind you as you head out for the day. Continue paying attention to the soundtrack of your life.

We are rarely good listeners. What I mean is that the one person we rarely listen to is ourselves. We tend to talk on autopilot. We do it without listening. When is the last time you really listened to yourself during a conversation with someone? On your listening day listen to you! What conversations are you not having? What is it that you do no hear yourself saying that you hoped you had the courage to say?

A day spent listening will shed some light on the thinking that goes on in the background. At the end of this day do you recognise the need to change the soundtrack of your life?

DAY 3 – TOUCH

Our third day is about how life feels to our touch. We live everyday and exist in this body of ours. Our bodies are covered with nerve endings to protect us from harm but also to help us feel alive and feel part of the world. However the feel of our life can be like an old pair of shoes: very familiar yet relatively unnoticed. I want to encourage you to begin again feeling the world.

Change the sheets. Put on fresh sheets the night before you go to bed. When you wake up be aware of how the fresh cotton or linen feels against your skin. Feel the temperature change as you get out of bed. What is the texture of the floor on your bare feet? Really be present to your shower. Take the time to fully be with the experience. Bring your full attention to how your day feels.

How does it feel as you step outside in to the bright morning light or maybe dark winter morning? Notice how you feel as you go through your day. If you meet someone and shake their hands or give them a hug be really present to the experience. Feel and recognise how important it is to be present and engaged with your physical world. Slow down and rush a little less through your day. If it takes 20 minutes to walk to work take 30. Don't use the elevator rather take the stairs and count how many there are. Notice how close you stand with people. Recognise what your comfort zone and personal space looks like. Let someone into your personal space and begin to be more connected with the world on this special day.

DAY 4 – TASTE

Day four is about the taste of life. What is your first taste sensation when you awake in the morning? Are you someone who has to reach for the coffee to kick start the day? Plan breakfast this special morning and allow yourself enough time to enjoy the experience. This is a special day in which to savour every flavour.

When you get to work or college organise a special lunch in your favourite café or restaurant and invite someone along. Order something unusual from the menu and relish the experience. Try and remember when you have had a memorable lunch before. Are you someone who rushes their food or skips lunch because there just isn't enough time? Leave the fast food world alone for this day.

Leave work early and go home to cook dinner. Invite some friends over and have a small celebration for no particular reason at all. Open a bottle of your favourite wine and savour every last drop. Notice how on other days you may have rushed through the taste of your life. Take time to experience the sensation that the flavour of life has to offer.

DAY 5 – SMELL

Our senses not only are there to help us engage with the world they play an important role in our thinking and choices we make. Walk into any supermarket and you will normally be met with the smell of freshly baked bread or often the flower stand. Our sense of smell is connected very strongly to our thinking. Recognising a familiar odour is a great way of triggering a particular memory. The latest research into Parkinson and Alzheimer's disease has suggested that a diminished sense of smell is and early indicator of the early onset of these diseases.

The perfume industry knows how important our sense of smell is. They have developed a billion pound industry on the science of attraction and emotion. The Real Estate industry knows that the smell of fresh coffee brewing during an open house sets the right tone. On this special day notice how your world appears to your sense of smell. Open all the windows in the house and let some fresh air in. Buy a new freshener for your car. Wear some of your favourite aftershave or perfume.

If you are having lunch in a restaurant smell your food for a change. Notice what memories the different smells evoke. Live a bit more in each moment of this day and recognise how often you may just be on autopilot.

DAY 6 - SILENCE

There was a patient in a mental hospital who stood most of the day with their ear up against the wall. One day a visitor asked him what he was doing. He replied "I am listening to the silence!" The visitor put his ear up against the wall and after a while said to the patient "I can't hear anything!" The patient replied, "Yes it's like that all the time!"

It is important to spend this last day on your own. One of the main casualties of modern life is silence. Living in the 21st Century makes most of us strangers to silence. Silence no longer appears to be there. Noise has become the default. Silence has now to be sought.

All the great mystical traditions have had silence at the centre of their spiritual practices. Silence is often what speaks loudest when we have no words to express our true feelings.

Silence will change you more than anything else. Christina Feldman in her book *Silence* says that silence asks us to see ourselves and the world with fresh eyes.

Silence can be incredibly difficult. This maybe the one day's exercise that really challenges us all. Silence highlights the struggle between the ego and the real you. The ego will want to distract us, rate our success, and challenge our ability to be still. The silent person within us may also be a relative stranger to us all.

So on your fifth day seek out somewhere you can be alone, somewhere to be with your own thoughts. Observe what is going on in your mind but don't try to chase or control any of the thoughts. See where this day takes you. What new thoughts have emerged? Have you glimpsed possibilities you never considered before?

Spending these days doing the exercises will begin to help you recognise and engage with your life in a new and richer way. It will help you turn off the autopilot and connect more fully with reality. These exercises are about raising awareness, awareness of reality, your reality.

Chapter Twenty-two
A NEW BEGINNING

"Our only security is our ability to change."
– John Lilly

This book is about taking you on a journey: a journey based on the simple model set out in the first part of this book. The journey began with presenting you with some random thoughts about; the lost submarine, the farmer's daughter, the tourist whose car broke down, and the violinist.

It then got your attention and showed you how powerful marketing; the environment; the people we spend time with; and our relationship with time play in all our lives.

Looking at stories about the fisherman and the Harvard Consultant; the lady and her cookies; and what the multinationals are doing to target our children.

Hopefully these stories got you emotionally engaged.

You faced a decision, a decision to continue with the book and undertake the 6 days of exercise which took a real commitment.

If you made that decision then you have moved to action. That action was to do the exercises.

Based on this understanding and new skills you have acquired you are prepared to begin living a more discerning and fulfilled life. Recognise that you are not there! This is only the beginning of a journey we are all on. You may have just started to dip your toe in the water of new experiences. Being human and alive is a great gift, one we can often take for granted. Being fully alive, being real, is hard work but it's the only worthwhile path. Recognise life offers us great opportunities to be the best we can. Today is always the best place to start to be who you really are.

EPILOGUE

"If all the world is a stage, where is the audience sitting?"
— Steve Wright

Life is amazing. Being fully alive involves getting excited about being here and remaining excited about the experience. We can choose to fight life or to engage fully with it.

The quality of our thinking impacts on the quality of our engagement with this wonderful everyday experience. However if we rely on how we feel at a particular moment in time to drive the choices we make, our lives may become chaotic.

Every action begins with a thought. It is our thinking that dictates the quality of our actions. Following our emotions, whims or desires is not living. If you do not make decisions based on principals or quality thinking then you may be blown about in life like a feather in the wind. It's a choice we all have to make.

Remember we are all just visitors to this planet we call Earth. None of us have been here before. As someone once said we are all in the play but no one has read the script.

Life whilst amazing is also unpredictable. We in truth have little control over events. What we do have control over is how we think and how we react to those events. Everyday offers us new challenges and experiences. We can look at life as a struggle to be endured or an amazing adventure to be enjoyed.

Thinking well is challenging, but we humans love a challenge. We have to remember that the joy is to be found in the journey.

Changing how you think will always change your life for the better. Changing how you think will allow you to live the life you always hoped and dreamed you could. So the next time life throws you a curve ball recognise that you have the knowledge, skills and the capacity to deal with it and that you are much more capable than you think you are.

References

Awareness	*Anthony De Mello 1990*
The Lucifer Effect	*Philip Zimbardo 2007*
Man's Search for Meaning	*Victor Frankl 1946*
BBC news website	*Andrew Bomford 2013*
Forgive for God	*Fred Luskin 2001*
To Have or to Be	*Erich Fromm 1976*
Joshua Bell	*The Washington Post 2007*
John O'Donohue	*Talk at Greenbelt Festival 2004*